The Super Easy

Ninja Foodi Cookbook

2000 Days of Bold and Brilliant Ninja Foodi Recipes to Cook Like a Pro \ Full Color Edition

Adrienne S. Mackey

Editor: AALIYAH LYONS

Interior Design: BROOKE WHITE

Cover Art: DANIELLE REES

Food stylist: Sienna Adams

Table Of Contents

Introduction

Welcome to the world of culinary innovation, where the ordinary becomes extraordinary and the kitchen transforms into a realm of endless possibilities. As you embark on this culinary journey, guided by the pages of this Ninja Foodi cookbook, prepare to elevate your cooking experience to new heights. The Ninja Foodi is not just an appliance; it's a game-changer, a versatile kitchen companion that unlocks a realm of culinary creativity.

In the fast-paced modern world, where time is a precious commodity, the Ninja Foodi stands as a beacon of efficiency. It's more than just a pressure cooker, more than an air fryer—it's a culinary powerhouse that seamlessly blends various cooking techniques into a single, sleek appliance. As a chef, home cook, or anyone with a passion for delicious and convenient meals, the Ninja Foodi is your secret weapon.

Picture this: succulent, fall-off-the-bone ribs infused with smoky flavors, achieved in a fraction of the time it would take with traditional methods. Imagine crispy, golden-brown chicken wings that rival your favorite sports bar's signature dish, but with a healthier twist thanks to the magic of air frying. The Ninja Foodi isn't just about speed; it's about unlocking flavors, textures, and culinary experiences that will leave your taste buds dancing.

In the pages that follow, you'll find a treasure trove of recipes meticulously crafted to showcase the Ninja Foodi's capabilities. From quick weeknight dinners to impressive Sunday feasts, each recipe is a testament to the versatility of this culinary marvel. But beyond the recipes, this cookbook is a guide—a roadmap to inspire your culinary creativity and empower you to experiment in the kitchen with newfound confidence.

The Ninja Foodi isn't just a tool; it's an enabler of culinary exploration. As you delve into the recipes, you'll discover the joy of experimenting with different cooking techniques, flavors, and ingredients. This isn't just about following instructions; it's about making each recipe your own, adapting and tweaking to suit your taste and preferences.

But the journey doesn't stop in the kitchen. The Ninja Foodi is a gateway to a healthier lifestyle, offering the ability to create delicious meals with less oil and more wholesome ingredients. It's about striking that perfect balance between indulgence and well-being, proving that you don't have to compromise taste for health.

Whether you're a seasoned chef or a kitchen novice, the Ninja Foodi is here to make your culinary dreams a reality. So, buckle up and get ready to embark on a delicious adventure. Let this cookbook be your guide, your companion in the kitchen, as you unleash the full potential of the Ninja Foodi and discover the joy of creating mouthwatering meals that will leave a lasting impression on your palate and those lucky enough to share in your culinary creations.

Happy cooking!

Chapter 1

Getting to Know Your Ninja Foodi

Features and Functions

In the bustling world of modern kitchens, the Ninja Foodi emerges as a culinary powerhouse, seamlessly blending various cooking functions into a single, sleek appliance. As we embark on a journey through the labyrinth of features and functions that define the Ninja Foodi, we discover a tool that not only simplifies cooking but elevates it to an art form.

PRESSURE COOKING MASTERY

At the heart of the Ninja Foodi lies its mastery of pressure cooking. This feature allows you to tenderize meats, infuse flavors, and accelerate cooking times, turning hours-long braises into mere minutes. The sealed environment traps steam, creating a high-pressure environment that results in succulent and flavorful dishes. From soups and stews to risottos and roasts, the Ninja Foodi's pressure cooking capabilities open a world of possibilities for both novice and experienced chefs.

AIR FRYING EXCELLENCE

Step into the realm of guilt-free indulgence with the Ninja Foodi's air frying prowess. This function harnesses the power of hot air circulation to create a crispy, golden exterior while maintaining the juiciness within. Whether you're craving classic fries, chicken wings, or even donuts, the air fryer function delivers a satisfying crunch without the need for excessive oil. It's a game-changer for those seeking a healthier approach to their favorite fried delights.

VERSATILITY WITH MULTIPLE COOKING MODES

The Ninja Foodi isn't content with being a one-trick pony. Its versatility extends beyond pressure cooking and air frying, incorporating various cooking modes to suit your culinary needs. From slow cooking for rich, savory stews to sautéing for perfectly caramelized vegetables, and baking for delectable desserts—the Ninja Foodi seamlessly transitions between modes, allowing you to prepare entire meals without the need for multiple appliances.

TENDERCRISP™ TECHNOLOGY

A groundbreaking innovation, the Ninja Foodi's TenderCrisp™ technology is a culinary revelation. This feature combines the best of both worlds—pressure cooking and air frying—to produce meals with a perfect balance of tenderness and crispiness. Picture a succulent roast with a crispy, golden-brown exterior, or juicy chicken thighs with irresistibly crispy skin. TenderCrisp™ technology ensures that your dishes are not only cooked to perfection but also boast a delightful textural contrast.

SMART COOKING WITH PRECISION CONTROL

The Ninja Foodi empowers you with precise control over the cooking process. Whether it's adjusting temperature settings, monitoring pressure levels, or setting precise cooking times, the appliance puts you in the driver's seat. The intuitive control panel and digital display make it easy to navigate through functions, giving you the confidence to experiment with recipes and customize cooking parameters to suit your taste.

EASY CLEANING WITH DISHWASHER-SAFE COMPONENTS

In the midst of culinary exploration, the last thing you want is a mountain of dishes. The Ninja Foodi acknowledges this and comes equipped with dishwasher-safe components, easing the cleanup process. The cooking pot, air fryer basket, and other accessories can be effortlessly cleaned in the dishwasher, allowing you to savor the joy of cooking without the burden of extensive post-meal cleanup.

Tips for Using the Ninja Foodi Efficiently

Embarking on a culinary journey with the Ninja Foodi is an exciting endeavor that promises efficiency without compromising flavor or creativity. To make the most of this versatile kitchen companion, consider the following tips for using the Ninja Foodi efficiently.

UNDERSTAND YOUR COOKING MODES

The Ninja Foodi boasts an array of cooking modes, from pressure cooking to air frying, sautéing, baking, and more. Understanding each mode's strengths and applications is key to unlocking the full potential of your appliance. Dive into the user manual, experiment with different modes, and gradually develop a sense of when to use each one. This knowledge will empower you to create a diverse range of dishes with precision.

MAXIMIZE DUAL FUNCTIONALITY

One of the standout features of the Ninja Foodi is its ability to seamlessly transition between pressure cooking and air frying with its TenderCrisp™ technology. Leverage this dual functionality to achieve the perfect balance of tenderness and crispiness in your dishes. For example, start by pressure cooking a hearty stew and finish it off with a quick air fry for a golden, crispy topping. This synergy opens up a world of culinary possibilities.

LAYER FLAVORS STRATEGICALLY

The Ninja Foodi allows you to layer flavors and textures in a single pot, enhancing the complexity of your dishes. When pressure cooking, consider placing ingredients with longer cooking times at the bottom and quicker-cooking items on top. This strategic layering ensures that each component is cooked to perfection, contributing to a harmonious and well-balanced final result.

PREHEAT FOR OPTIMAL RESULTS

Just like with traditional ovens, preheating your Ninja Foodi is a valuable step for achieving optimal results. Preheating ensures that the cooking chamber is at the right temperature from the start, leading to more consistent and efficient cooking. For air frying, this step is particularly crucial to achieving that coveted crispy texture.

UTILIZE THE REVERSIBLE RACK

Many Ninja Foodi models come with a reversible rack, offering two cooking levels. Take advantage of this feature to cook multiple items simultaneously, saving time and energy. For example, use the rack to elevate proteins while vegetables cook below, ensuring a well-rounded meal with minimal effort.

OPT FOR BATCH COOKING

Embrace the efficiency of batch cooking with the Ninja Foodi. Prepare larger quantities of your favorite dishes and store leftovers for later meals. Not only does this save time on future cooking sessions, but it also ensures that you have convenient and delicious options on hand for busy days.

EMBRACE ONE-POT WONDERS

The Ninja Foodi is a champion of one-pot wonders. Experiment with recipes that allow you to throw all your ingredients into the pot for a hassle-free cooking experience. From soups and stews to casseroles and risottos, the Ninja Foodi's even cooking and versatile modes make it an ideal tool for creating flavorful one-pot meals.

EXPERIMENT WITH TIME AND TEMPERATURE

Precision control is at your fingertips with the Ninja Foodi, so don't hesitate to experiment with cooking times and temperatures. Tailor recipes to your taste preferences and adjust settings based on the texture you desire. Over time, you'll develop an intuitive sense of how the Ninja Foodi responds to different settings, giving you unparalleled control in the kitchen.

As we conclude this culinary odyssey with the Ninja Foodi, we've unlocked the potential of a kitchen companion that goes beyond efficiency—it's a creative force. Armed with an understanding of its features, efficiency tips, and essential kitchen tools, you're poised to embark on a flavorful journey. The Ninja Foodi isn't just a time-saver; it's a gateway to culinary exploration. May your kitchen be filled with the sizzles, aromas, and delights that only the Ninja Foodi can deliver. Happy cooking, and may every meal be a testament to your culinary prowess!

Chapter 2

Breakfast Recipes

Healthy Carrot Breakfast Bars

Prep time: 5 minutes | Cook time: 30 minutes |Serves 16

- 1/2 cup whole wheat flour
- 1 tsp cinnamon
- 1 tsp baking soda
- 1 1/2 cups rolled oats
- 2 tbsp flaxseed meal
- 1 cup carrot, grated
- 1/4 cup maple syrup
- 1/4 cup mashed banana
- 1 tsp vanilla
- 1/2 cup almond butter
- 3/4 cup milk

1. In a mixing bowl, whisk milk, butter, vanilla, mashed banana, maple syrup, carrot, and flaxseed meal.
2. Add oats, flour, cinnamon, and baking soda and mix until well combined.
3. Pour mixture into the greased baking pan.
4. Select bake mode then set the temperature to 350 F and time for 30 minutes. Press start.
5. Once the oven is preheated then place the baking pan into the oven.
6. Slice and serve.

Cinnamon Sugar Donuts

Prep time: 10 minutes | Cook time: 5 minutes Serves8

- 450g refrigerated flaky jumbo biscuits
- ½ cup granulated white sugar
- 2 teaspoons ground cinnamon
- 4 tablespoons butter, melted
- Olive oil spray

1. Combine the sugar and cinnamon in a bowl; leave aside.
2. Take the biscuits out of the can, divide them, and lay them out on a flat surface. Make holes in each biscuit with a 1-inch-round biscuit cutter.
3. Using an olive or coconut oil spray, lightly coat the roast tray.
4. In the roast tray, arrange 4 doughnuts in a single layer. Make certain they aren't in contact.
5. Turn on your Ninja Foodi and select "Bake".
6. Select the timer for 5 minutes and the temperature for 360 °F.
7. When the unit beeps to show that it has preheated, open the oven and insert the roast tray on sheet pan into the rail of Level 3 in oven.
8. Serve and enjoy!

Ham and Cheese Scones

Prep time: 15 minutes | Cook time: 25 minutes | Serves 6

- 2 cups all-purpose flour
- 1 tablespoon baking powder
- 2 teaspoons sugar
- 1 teaspoon kosher salt
- 2 tablespoons butter, cubed
- 1 cup ham, diced, cooked
- 4 ounces cheddar cheese, shredded
- ¼ cup milk
- ¾ cup heavy cream

1. Whisk baking powder with flour, sugar, salt, and butter in a mixing bowl.
2. Beat milk, cream, and all other ingredients in another bowl.
3. Stir in the flour-butter mixture and mix well until it forms a smooth dough.
4. Place this scones dough on a floured surface and spread it into a 7-inch round sheet.
5. Cut this dough sheet into 6 wedges of equal size.
6. Place these wedges in the cooking pan, lined with parchment paper.
7. When baked, serve the scones with morning eggs.

Savory French Toast

Prep time: 10 minutes | Cook time: 5 minutes | Serves 2

- ¼ cup chickpea flour
- 3 tablespoons onion, finely chopped
- 2 teaspoons green chili, seeded and finely chopped
- ½ teaspoon red chili powder
- ¼ teaspoon ground turmeric
- ¼ teaspoon ground cumin
- salt, to taste
- water, as needed
- 4 bread slices

1. Add all the ingredients except bread slices in a large bowl and mix until a thick mixture form.
2. with a spoon, spread the mixture over both sides of each bread slice.
3. Arrange the bread slices into the lightly greased sheet pan.
4. Press "Power" button of Ninja Foodi and turn the dial to select "Air Fry" mode.
5. Press TIME/SLICE button and again turn the dial to set the cooking time to 5 minutes
6. When cooking time is completed, open the oven door and serve warm.

Pancetta & Spinach Frittata

Prep time: 15 minutes | Cook time: 16 minutes

Serves2

- ¼ cup pancetta
- ½ of tomato, cubed
- ¼ cup fresh baby spinach
- 3 eggs
- Salt and ground black pepper, as required
- ¼ cup Parmesan cheese, grated

1. Heat a nonstick skillet over medium heat and cook the pancetta for about 5 minutes.
2. Add the tomato and spinach cook for about 2-3 minutes.
3. Remove from the heat and drain the grease from skillet.
4. Set aside to cool slightly.
5. When cooking time is completed, open the oven door, and remove the pan.
6. Cut into equal-sized wedges and serve.

Breakfast Pizzas with Muffins

Prep time: 5 minutes | Cook time: 6 minutes | Serves 3

- 6 eggs, cooked and scrambled
- 1 pound ground sausage
- ½ cup Colby jack cheese, shredded
- 3 egg muffins, sliced in half
- olive oil spray

1. Using olive oil cooking spray, spray the air fry basket.
2. Place each half in the basket.
3. Using a light layer of olive oil spray, lightly coat the English muffins and top with scrambled eggs and fried sausages.
4. Add cheese on top of each one.
5. Turn on your Ninja Foodi and rotate the knob to select "Bake".
6. Select the timer for 5 minutes and the temperature for 355 °F.
7. Serve hot.

Zucchini Fritters

Prep time: 15 minutes | Cook time: 7 minutes | Serves 4

- 10½ ounces zucchini, grated and squeezed
- 7 ounces Halloumi cheese
- ¼ cup all-purpose flour
- 2 eggs
- 1 teaspoon fresh dill, minced
- salt and ground black pepper, as required

1. In a large bowl and mix all the ingredients together.
2. Make small-sized fritters from the mixture.
3. Press "Power" button of Ninja Foodi and turn the dial to select "Air Fry" mode.
4. Press TIME/SLICE button and again turn the dial to set the cooking time to 7 minutes
5. Now push TEMP/DARKNESS button and rotate the dial to set the temperature at 355 °F.
6. Press "Start/Pause" button to start.
7. When the unit beeps to show that it is preheated, open the oven door.
8. Arrange fritters into the greased sheet pan and insert in the oven.
9. When cooking time is completed, open the oven door and serve warm.

French Toast Casserole

Prep time: 10 minutes | Cook time: 12 minutes | Serves 6

- 3 large eggs
- 1 cup whole milk
- ¼ teaspoon kosher salt or ⅛ teaspoon fine salt
- 1 tablespoon pure maple syrup
- 1 teaspoon vanilla
- ¼ teaspoon cinnamon
- 3 cups (1-inch) stale bread cubes (3 to 4 slices)
- 1 tablespoon unsalted butter, at room temperature

1. In a medium bowl, whisk the eggs until the yolks and whites are completely mixed. Add the milk, salt, maple syrup, vanilla, and cinnamon and whisk to combine. Add the bread cubes and gently stir to coat with the egg mixture. Let sit for 2 to 3 minutes so the bread absorbs some of the custard, then gently stir again.
2. Grease the bottom of the sheet pan with the butter. Pour the bread mixture onto the pan, spreading it out evenly.
3. When cooking is complete, serve warm with additional butter and maple syrup, if desired.

Easy Maple-Glazed Doughnuts

Prep time: 10 minutes | Cook time: 14 minutes |Serves 8

- 1 (8-count) can jumbo flaky refrigerator biscuits
- ½ cup light brown sugar
- 2 cups confectioners' sugar, plus more for dusting (optional)
- 2 teaspoons pure maple syrup

1. Insert the crisper plate into the basket and the basket into the unit. Preheat the unit by selecting AIR FRY, setting the temperature to 350°F, and setting the time to 3 minutes. Select START/STOP to begin.
2. Remove the biscuits from the tube and cut out the center of each biscuit with a small, round cookie cutter.
3. Once the unit is preheated, spray the crisper plate with cooking oil. Working in batches, place 4 doughnuts into the basket.
4. Dip the slightly cooled doughnuts into the maple glaze. Place them on a wire rack and dust with confectioners' sugar (if using). Let rest just until the glaze sets. Enjoy the doughnuts warm.

Delicious Potato Casserole

Prep time: 5 minutes | Cook time: 35 minutes |Serves 10

- 7 eggs
- 1/2 cup almond milk
- 1 onion, chopped & sautéed
- 8 oz cheddar cheese, grated
- 20 oz frozen hash browns, diced
- 1 lb sausage, cooked
- Pepper
- Salt

1. Place rack in the bottom position and close door. Select bake mode set the temperature to 350 F and set the timer to 35 minutes. Press the setting dial to preheat.
2. In a mixing bowl, whisk eggs with milk, pepper, and salt.
3. Add remaining ingredients and mix well.
4. Pour egg mixture into the prepared casserole dish.
5. Once the unit is preheated, open the door, and place the casserole dish onto the center of the rack, and close the door.
6. Serve and enjoy.

Homemade Strawberry Breakfast Tarts

Prep time: 15 minutes | Cook time: 10 minutes |Serves 6

- 2 refrigerated piecrusts
- ½ cup strawberry preserves
- 1 teaspoon cornstarch
- Cooking oil spray
- ½ cup low-fat vanilla yogurt
- 1 ounce cream cheese, at room temperature
- 3 tablespoons confectioners' sugar
- Rainbow sprinkles, for decorating

1. Place the piecrusts on a flat surface. Using a knife or pizza cutter, cut each piecrust into 3 rectangles, for 6 total. Discard any unused dough from the piecrust edges.
2. In a small bowl, stir together the preserves and cornstarch. Mix well, ensuring there are no lumps of cornstarch remaining.
3. Scoop 1 tablespoon of the strawberry mixture onto the top half of each piece of piecrust.
4. In a small bowl, stir together the yogurt, cream cheese, and confectioners' sugar. Spread the breakfast tarts with the frosting and top with sprinkles.

Sweet & Spiced Toasts

Prep time: 10 minutes | Cook time: 4 minutes | Serves 3

- ¼ cup sugar
- ½ teaspoon ground cinnamon
- ⅛ teaspoon ground cloves
- ⅛ teaspoon ground ginger
- ½ teaspoons vanilla extract
- ¼ cup salted butter, softened
- 6 bread slices

1. In a bowl, add the sugar, vanilla, cinnamon, pepper, and butter. Mix until smooth.
2. Spread the butter mixture evenly over each bread slice.
3. Press "Power Button" of Ninja Foodi and select "Air Fry" function.
4. Press "Temp Button" to set the temperature at 400 °F.
5. Now press "time Button" to set the cooking time to 4 minutes.
6. Press "START/STOP" button to start.
7. When the unit beeps to show that it is preheated, open the lid and grease the air fry basket.
8. When cooking time is completed, open the lid and transfer the French toasts onto a platter.
9. Serve warm.

German Pancake

Prep time: 5 minutes | Cook time: 30 minutes

Serves8

- 6 large eggs
- 1 cup 2% milk
- 1 cup all-purpose flour
- ½ teaspoon salt
- 2 tablespoons butter, melted
- Powdered sugar, for serving
- ½ cup butter
- 1½ cups sugar
- ¾ cup buttermilk
- 2 tablespoons corn syrup
- 1 teaspoon baking soda
- 2 teaspoons vanilla extract

1. Insert a wire rack on level 3 in your oven. Select the BAKE function, 400°F, for 30 minutes. While the oven is preheating, prepare the ingredients.
2. Put the eggs, 2% milk, flour, and salt in a blender and blend until smooth.
3. Pour the melted butter into an oven-safe baking dish and coat the surface. Then add the batter.
4. Cook for about 7 minutes, then remove from the heat and stir in the vanilla extract.
5. Take out the pancake and sprinkle it with confectioners' sugar.

Everything Bagels

Prep time: 10 minutes | Cook time: 10 minutes

|Serves 2

- ½ cup self-rising flour, plus more for dusting
- ½ cup plain Greek yogurt
- 1 egg
- 1 tablespoon water
- 4 teaspoons everything bagel spice mix
- 1 tablespoon butter, melted

1. In a large bowl, using a wooden spoon, stir together the flour and yogurt until a tacky dough forms. Transfer the dough to a lightly floured work surface and roll the dough into a ball.
2. Cut the dough into 2 pieces and roll each piece into a log. Form each log into a bagel shape, pinching the ends together.
3. In a small bowl, whisk the egg and water. Brush the egg wash on the bagels.
4. Sprinkle 2 teaspoons of the spice mix on each bagel and gently press it into the dough.
5. Select BAKE, set the temperature to 330°F, and set the time to 10 minutes. Select START/STOP to begin.
6. When the cooking is complete, the bagels should be lightly golden on the outside. Serve warm.

Classic Corned Beef Hash and Eggs

Prep time: 10 minutes | Cook time: 12 minutes | Serves 4

- 2 medium Yukon Gold potatoes, peeled, cut into ¼-inch cubes (about 3 cups)
- 1 medium onion, chopped (about 1 cup)
- ⅓ cup diced red bell pepper
- 3 tablespoons vegetable oil
- ½ teaspoon dried thyme
- ½ teaspoon kosher salt or ¼ teaspoon fine salt, divided
- ½ teaspoon freshly ground black pepper, divided
- ¾ pound corned beef, cut into ¼-inch pieces
- 4 large eggs

1. In a large bowl, mix the potatoes, onion, red pepper, oil, thyme, ¼ teaspoon of salt, and ¼ teaspoon of pepper. Spread the vegetables on the sheet pan in an even layer.
2. Once the unit has preheated, slide the sheet pan into the oven.
3. When cooking is complete, remove the pan from the oven. Serve immediately.

Sweet Potato Breakfast Bake

Prep time: 5 minutes | Cook time: 60 minutes |Serves 8

- 3 eggs
- 3/4 tsp cinnamon
- 1/4 cup coconut flour
- 1/4 cup raisins
- 1 mashed banana
- 1/3 cup maple syrup
- 2 sweet potatoes, peel & grated
- 1/4 tsp salt

1. In a large bowl, add mashed banana, eggs, maple syrup, raisins, and sweet potatoes and mix well.
2. Add cinnamon, coconut flour, and salt and mix until well combined.
3. Pour mixture into the greased baking dish.
4. Select bake mode then set the temperature to 350 F and time for 60 minutes. Press start.
5. Once the oven is preheated then place the baking dish into the oven.
6. Slice and serve.

Chapter 3

Snacks and Appetizer Recipes

Zucchini Crisps

**Prep time: 5 minutes | Cook time: 30 minutes
|Serves 2**

- 2 larges zucchinis cut in sticks or round
- salt, to taste
- 1 cup all-purpose flour
- 2 ½ cups bread crumbs
- ⅓ cup Parmesan cheese, grated
- 1 tablespoon garlic powder
- 1 teaspoon onion powder

1. Put zucchini in a bowl and add salt; let it sit for a while to drain excess liquid.
2. In a medium-sized bowl, mix the cheese, garlic powder, bread crumbs, onion powder, and salt. Whisk the eggs in a bowl.
3. Place flour in a shallow bowl separately. Toss zucchini in egg wash, then in flour, and at the end in bread crumb mixture.
4. Halfway through, toss the zucchini.
5. Once it's done, serve.

Chipotle Potato Fries

**Prep time: 5 minutes | Cook time: 25 minutes
|Serves 6**

- 2 sweet potatoes, cut into fries shape
- 1/4 tsp pepper
- 1/2 tsp chipotle chili powder
- 1/2 tsp paprika
- 2 tbsp olive oil
- Salt

1. Add sweet potato fries, pepper, chili powder, paprika, oil, and salt into the large bowl and toss well.
2. Spray sheet pan with cooking spray.
3. Spread sweet potato fries on a greased sheet pan.
4. Select bake mode then set the temperature to 450 F and time for 25 minutes. Press start.
5. Once the oven is preheated then place the sheet pan into the oven.
6. Stir fries after 15 minutes.
7. Serve and enjoy.

Easy Roasted Peanuts

Prep time: 5 minutes | Cook time: 14 minutes |Serves 6

- 1 ½ cups raw peanuts
- Nonstick cooking spray

1. Turn on your Ninja Foodi and select the "AIR CRISP" function.
2. Set the temperature at 320 °F and cooking time to 14 minutes.
3. Press the "START/PAUSE" button to start. When the unit beeps to show that it is preheated, open the door.
4. Arrange the peanuts in the Air Crisp Basket and insert them in the oven.
5. While cooking, toss the peanuts twice. After 9 minutes of cooking, spray the peanuts with cooking spray.
6. When cooking time is completed, open the door and transfer the peanuts into a heatproof bowl.
7. Serve warm.

Spicy Carrot Fries

Prep time: 10 minutes | Cook time: 12 minutes | Serves 2

- 1 large carrot, peeled and cut into sticks
- 1 tablespoon fresh rosemary, chopped finely
- 1 tablespoon olive oil
- ¼ teaspoon cayenne pepper
- salt and ground black pepper, as required

1. In a bowl, add all the ingredients and mix well.
2. Press "Power" button of Ninja Foodi and turn the dial to select "Air Fry" mode.
3. Press TIME/SLICE button and again turn the dial to set the cooking time to 12 minutes
4. When cooking time is completed, open the oven door and transfer the carrot fries onto a platter.
5. Serve warm.

Tofu Nuggets

Prep time: 10 minutes | Cook time: 15 minutes
Serves4

- 400g extra firm tofu
- ⅓ cup nutritional yeast
- ¼ cup water
- 1 tablespoon garlic powder
- 1 teaspoon onion powder
- 1 teaspoon sweet paprika
- 1 teaspoon poultry spice

1. Press the tofu for 10 minutes.
2. Add all ingredients to a bowl and stir to combine.
3. Over the bowl, break the tofu into bite-sized chunks. Use your thumb to create rough, rounded edges as you go.
4. Fold the chunks into the paste gently, taking care not to break the tofu.
5. Place the tofu in air fry basket in a single layer.
6. Turn on Ninja Foodi and select "Air Fry".
7. Select the timer for 15 minutes and the temperature for 350 °F.
8. Halfway through, pause and shake the basket. Serve immediately or save for later.

Classic French Fries

Prep time: 35 minutes | Cook time: 30 minutes
|Serves 6

- 3 large russet potatoes, peeled and cut lengthwise into fry shapes
- 1 tablespoon canola oil
- 1 tablespoon extra-virgin olive oil
- Salt
- Freshly ground black pepper
- Fresh parsley, for garnish (optional)

1. Place the potatoes in a large bowl of cold water and let soak for at least 30 minutes, preferably 1 hour (see Ingredient Tip). Drain the potatoes and thoroughly dry them using a clean kitchen towel.
2. Insert the crisper plate into the basket and the basket into the unit. Preheat the unit by selecting AIR FRY, setting the temperature to 390°F, and setting the time to 3 minutes. Select START/STOP to begin.
3. When the second batch is complete, return all the fries to the basket and shake it. Air fry for 1 minute more so all the fries are hot before serving. Garnish with chopped parsley (if using).

Eggplant Fries

Prep time: 15 minutes | Cook time: 10 minutes | Serves 4

- 2 large eggs
- ½ cup grated Parmesan cheese
- ½ cup toasted wheat germ
- 1 teaspoon Italian seasoning
- ¾ teaspoon garlic salt
- 1 (1¼-pound) eggplant, peeled
- cooking spray
- 1 cup meatless pasta sauce, warmed

1. Cut the eggplant into sticks.
2. Mix parmesan cheese, wheat germ, seasoning, and garlic salt in a bowl.
3. Coat the eggplant sticks with the parmesan mixture.
4. Transfer the basket to the Ninja Foodi and close the door.
5. Press Start/Pause to begin cooking.
6. Serve warm with marinara sauce.

Delicious Bean Dip

Prep time: 5 minutes | Cook time: 25 minutes |Serves 8

- 32 oz can refried beans
- 1 cup Monterey jack cheese, shredded
- 1 cup cheddar cheese, shredded
- 1 oz taco seasoning
- 1 cup sour cream
- 8 oz cream cheese, softened

1. Add refried beans and remaining ingredients into the large mixing bowl and mix until well combined.
2. Pour mixture into the greased baking dish.
3. Select bake mode then set the temperature to 350 F and time for 25 minutes. Press start.
4. Once the oven is preheated then place the baking dish into the oven.
5. Serve and enjoy.

Air-Fried Spring Rolls

Prep time: 10 minutes | Cook time: 9 minutes |Serves 16

- 4 teaspoons toasted sesame oil
- 6 medium garlic cloves, minced or pressed
- 1 tablespoon grated peeled fresh ginger
- 2 cups thinly sliced shiitake mushrooms
- 4 cups chopped green cabbage
- 1 cup grated carrot
- ½ teaspoon sea salt
- 16 rice paper wrappers

1. Place a wok or sauté pan over medium heat until hot.
2. Add the sesame oil, garlic, ginger, mushrooms, cabbage, carrot, and salt. Cook for 3 to 4 minutes, stirring often, until the cabbage is lightly wilted. Remove the pan from the heat.
3. When the cooking is complete, the egg rolls should be crisp-ish and lightly browned. Serve immediately, plain or with a sauce of choice.

Ranch Kale Chips

Prep time: 15 minutes | Cook time: 5 minutes | Serves 6

- 2 tablespoons olive oil
- 4 cups kale leaves
- 2 teaspoons vegan ranch seasoning
- 1 tablespoon nutritional yeast flakes
- ¼ teaspoon salt

1. Toss the kale leaves with oil, yeast, and ranch seasoning in a large bowl.
2. Spread the seasoned kale leaves in the oven.
3. Transfer the sandwich to the 3rd rack position of Ninja Foodi and close the door.
4. Select the "Air Fry" Mode using the Function Keys and select Rack Level 3.
5. Set its cooking time to 5 minutes and temperature to 370 °F, then press "START/STOP" to initiate cooking.
6. Serve warm.

Persimmon Chips

Prep time: 10 minutes | Cook time: 10 minutes | Serves 2

- 2 ripe persimmons, cut into slices horizontally
- Salt and ground black pepper, as required

1. Arrange the persimmons slices onto the greased sheet pan.
2. Press "Power Button" of Ninja Foodi and select "Air Fry" function.
3. Press "Temp Button" to set the temperature at 400 °F.
4. Now press "time Button" to set the cooking time to 10 minutes.
5. Press "START/STOP" button to start.
6. When the unit beeps to show that it is preheated, open the lid.
7. Insert the sheet pan in oven.
8. Flip the chips once halfway through.
9. When cooking time is completed, open the lid and transfer the chips onto a platter.
10. Serve warm.

Air Fryer Ravioli

Prep time: 5 minutes | Cook time: 10 minutes | Serves 2

- 12 frozen ravioli
- ½ cup buttermilk
- ½ cup Italian breadcrumbs
- cooking oil

1. Place two bowls next to each other. In one, put the buttermilk, and in the other, put the breadcrumbs.
2. Dip Each ravioli piece in buttermilk and then breadcrumbs, making sure it is well coated.
3. Place each breaded ravioli in a single layer in the air fry basket and spritz the tops halfway through with oil.
4. Place it inside the oven.
5. Turn on Ninja Foodi and rotate the knob to select "Air Fry".
6. Select the timer for 7 minutes and the temperature for 400 °F.
7. Remove from the Ninja Foodi to serve hot.

Crispy Lemon-Pepper Wings

Prep time: 5 minutes | Cook time: 24 minutes | Serves 10

- 2 pounds chicken wing flats and drumettes (about 16 to 20 pieces)
- 1½ teaspoons kosher salt or ¾ teaspoon fine salt
- 4½ teaspoons salt-free lemon pepper seasoning (I use Penzey's Sunny Spain mix)
- Place the wings in a large bowl.

1. In a small bowl, stir together the salt, baking powder, and seasoning mix. Sprinkle the mixture over the wings and toss thoroughly to coat the wings. (This works best with your hands.) If you have time, let the wings sit for 20 to 30 minutes. Place the wings on the sheet pan, making sure they don't crowd each other too much.
2. Select AIR FRY, set temperature to 375°F, and set time to 24 minutes. Select START/PAUSE to begin preheating.
3. When cooking is complete, the wings should be dark golden brown and a bit charred in places. Remove the pan from the oven and let cool for before serving.

Chiles Rellenos–Style Nachos

Prep time: 10 minutes | Cook time: 10 minutes | Serves 6

- 8 ounces tortilla chips
- 3 cups shredded Monterey Jack cheese
- 1 (8-ounce) can tomato sauce
- ¼ teaspoon granulated garlic
- ¼ teaspoon dried oregano
- ¼ teaspoon freshly ground black pepper
- Pinch cinnamon
- Pinch cayenne pepper

1. Arrange the tortilla chips close together in a single layer on the sheet pan. Sprinkle half of the cheese over the chips. Arrange the green chiles over the cheese as evenly as possible, then cover with the remaining cheese.
2. Once the unit has preheated, slide the pan into the oven.
3. After 5 minutes, rotate the pan 180 degrees and continue cooking.
4. While the nachos are cooking, stir together the tomato sauce, garlic, oregano, pepper, cinnamon, and cayenne in a small bowl.

Chapter 4

Poultry Recipes

Gingered Chicken Drumsticks

Prep time: 10 minutes | Cook time: 25 minutes | Serves 3

- ¼ cup full-fat coconut milk
- 2 teaspoons fresh ginger, minced
- 2 teaspoons galangal, minced
- 2 teaspoons ground turmeric
- salt, as required
- 3 (6-ounce) chicken drumsticks

1. Place the coconut milk, galangal and spices in a large bowl and mix well.
2. Add the chicken drumsticks and coat with the marinade generously.
3. Refrigerate to marinate for at least 6-8 hours.
4. Press "Power" button of Ninja Foodi and turn the dial to select "Air Fry" mode.
5. Press TIME/SLICE button and again turn the dial to set the cooking time to 25 minutes
6. Now push TEMP/DARKNESS button and rotate the dial to set the temperature at 375 °F.
7. When cooking time is completed, open the oven door and serve hot.

Air Fryer Chicken Taco Pockets

Prep time: 5 minutes | Cook time: 25 minutes Serves8

- 2 8-ounce tubes of crescent rolls
- ½ cup salsa
- ½ cup sour cream
- 2 tablespoons taco seasoning
- 1 cup rotisserie chicken, shredded
- 1 cup cheddar cheese, shredded

1. Select the AIR FRY function, 375°F, for 15 minutes. While the oven is preheating, prepare the ingredients.
2. Unroll 1 tube of crescent roll, separate it into 2 rectangles, and press the perforation to seal. Repeat for the other tube.
3. Take a bowl, and combine the sour cream, salsa, and taco seasoning. Place some shredded chicken on the left sides of the rectangles and top them with the salsa mixture. Sprinkle with the cheese and fold the dough over the filling, then pinch the edges to seal.
4. Close the oven and cook for about 13 to 15 minutes. Cut in half and serve.

Oat Crusted Chicken Breasts

Prep time: 15 minutes | Cook time: 12 minutes | Serves 2

- 2 (6-ounce) chicken breasts
- Salt and ground black pepper, as required
- ¾ cup oats
- 2 tablespoons mustard powder
- 1 tablespoon fresh parsley
- 2 medium eggs

1. Check the meat "best by" date. Place the chicken breasts onto a cutting board and with a meat mallet, flatten each into even thickness.
2. Then, cut each breast in half.
3. Sprinkle the chicken pieces with salt and black pepper and set aside.
4. In a blender, add the oats, mustard powder, parsley, salt and black pepper and pulse until a coarse breadcrumb-like mixture is formed.
5. In another bowl, crack the eggs and beat well.
6. Coat the chicken with oats mixture and then, dip into beaten eggs and again, coat with the oats mixture.
7. When cooking time is completed, open the lid and serve hot.

Simple Chicken Thighs

Prep time: 5 minutes | Cook time: 20 minutes Serves4

- 4 skinless, boneless chicken thighs
- Salt and ground black pepper, as required
- 2 tablespoons butter, melted

1. Line a SearPlate with a lightly greased piece of foil.
2. Rub the chicken thighs with salt and black pepper evenly and then, brush with melted butter.
3. Place the chicken thighs into the prepared SearPlate.
4. Press AIR FRYER button of Ninja Foodi and turn the dial to select "Bake" mode.
5. Press TIME/SLICES button and again turn the dial to set the cooking time to 20 minutes.
6. Now push TEMP/SHADE button and rotate the dial to set the temperature at 450 °F.
7. Press "Start/Stop" button to start.
8. When the unit beeps to show that it is preheated, open the oven door and insert the SearPlate in oven.
9. When the cooking time is completed, open the oven door and serve hot.

Marinated Spicy Chicken Legs

Prep time: 10 minutes | Cook time: 20 minutes | Serves 4

- 4 chicken legs
- 3 tablespoons fresh lemon juice
- 3 teaspoons ginger paste
- 3 teaspoons garlic paste
- Salt, as required
- 4 tablespoons plain yogurt
- 2 teaspoons red chili powder
- 1 teaspoon ground cumin
- 1 teaspoon ground coriander
- 1 teaspoon ground turmeric
- Ground black pepper, as required

1. In a bowl, mix the chicken legs, lemon juice, ginger, garlic, and salt together. Set aside for about 15 minutes.
2. Meanwhile, in another bowl, mix the yogurt and spices together.
3. Add the chicken legs and coat with the spice mixture generously.
4. Cover the bowl and refrigerate for at least 10-12 hours.
5. When cooking time is completed, open the lid and serve hot.

Tasty Chicken Bites

Prep time: 5 minutes | Cook time: 20 minutes Serves4

- 2 lbs chicken thighs, cut into chunks
- 2 tbsp olive oil
- 1/2 tsp onion powder
- 1/2 tsp garlic powder
- 1/4 cup fresh lemon juice
- 1/4 tsp white pepper
- Pepper
- Salt

1. Select air fry mode set the temperature to 380 F and set the timer to 20 minutes. Press the setting dial to preheat.
2. Add chicken chunks and remaining ingredients into the large bowl and mix well.
3. Cover and place in refrigerator for overnight.
4. Arrange chicken in the air fryer basket.
5. Once the unit is preheated, open the door, and place the air fryer basket on the top level of the oven, and close the door.
6. Serve and enjoy.

Roasted Duck

Prep time: 15 minutes | Cook time: 3 hours | Serves 6

- 6 lbs. whole Pekin duck
- Salt, to taste
- 5 garlic cloves chopped
- 1 lemon, chopped
- Glaze
- ½ cup balsamic vinegar
- 1 lemon, juiced
- ¼ cup honey

1. Place the Pekin duck in a baking tray and add garlic, lemon, and salt on top.
2. Whisk honey, vinegar, and lemon juice in a bowl.
3. Select the "Air Roast" Mode using the Function Keys and select Rack Level 1.
4. Set its cooking time to 3 hours and temperature to 350 °F, then press "START/STOP" to initiate cooking.
5. Serve warm.

Thyme Roasted Chicken

Prep time: 5 minutes | Cook time: 5 hours Serves6

- 1 whole chicken
- 5 sprigs thyme, chopped
- 5 garlic cloves, crushed
- ¼ cup lemon juice
- 1 tablespoon canola oil
- ¼ cup honey
- 2 tablespoons salt
- 1 tablespoon pepper

1. Take the garlic cloves and push them into chicken cavities
2. Brush chicken with a mixture of lemon juice, honey, and oil on every side. Season with thyme, salt, and pepper
3. Transfer to your Ninja Foodi.
4. Press the "AIR ROAST" option and set it to 250 °F Cook for 5 hours
5. Serve and enjoy!

Braised Chicken with Polenta

Prep time: 10 minutes | Cook time: 27 minutes | Serves 4

- 4 bone-in, skin-on chicken thighs (about 1½ pounds)
- 1½ teaspoon kosher salt or ¾ teaspoon fine salt, divided
- Cooking oil spray
- 1 link sweet or hot Italian sausage (about ¼ pound), whole
- 1 tablespoon extra-virgin olive oil
- 4 hot or sweet pickled cherry peppers, seeded and quartered, along with 2 tablespoons pickling liquid from the jar
- ¼ cup low-sodium chicken stock
- 4 (1-inch) slices Oven Polenta

1. Salt the chicken thighs on both sides with 1 teaspoon of kosher salt. Spray the sheet pan with cooking oil spray and place the thighs skin-side down on the pan. Add the sausage.
2. Select AIR ROAST, set temperature to 375°F, and set time to 27 minutes. Select START/PAUSE to begin preheating.
3. Once the unit has preheated, slide the pan into the oven.

Korean-Style Fried Chicken

Prep time:20 minutes | Cook time: 35 minutes | Serves 4 to 6

- 1 (5-pound) whole chicken, cut into serving pieces (drumsticks, thighs, breasts)
- 2 tablespoons rice vinegar
- 2 tablespoons kosher salt
- 1 cup cornstarch
- ¼ cup honey
- 2 tablespoons soy sauce
- Canola oil cooking spray

1. In a large bowl, toss the chicken pieces with the rice vinegar, salt, pepper, and ginger. Working in batches, liberally coat all the pieces in the cornstarch, shaking off any excess. Set aside.
2. In a separate bowl, whisk together the honey, ketchup, chili paste, and soy sauce until smooth. Set aside.
3. Install a wire rack on Level 2. Select AIR FRY, set the temperature to 350°F, and set the time to 15 minutes. Press START/STOP to begin preheating.
4. Cooking is complete when an instant-read thermometer inserted into the chicken reads 165°F. Remove the chicken and immediately toss the pieces in the reserved sauce, or serve the sauce on the side. Serve immediately.

Roasted Turkey Breast

Prep time: 5 minutes | Cook time: 50 minutes Serves6

- 3pounds turkey breast, boneless
- ¼ cup mayonnaise
- 2 teaspoons poultry seasoning
- ¼ teaspoon pepper
- ½ teaspoon garlic powder
- 1 teaspoon salt

1. Whisk all the ingredients, including turkey, in a bowl, and coat it well.
2. Place the boneless turkey breast in the Air Fryer Basket.
3. Select "AIR CRISP" mode on your Ninja Foodi.
4. Set the cooking time to 50 minutes.
5. Now press the Temp button and rotate the dial to set the temperature at 350 °F.
6. Once preheated, place the Air Fryer basket in the Oven and Close its door to air fry.
7. Once done, slice and serve.

Buttermilk Whole Chicken

Prep time: 15 minutes | Cook time: 50 minutes | Serves 6

- 2 cups buttermilk
- ¼ cup olive oil
- 1 teaspoon garlic powder
- salt, as required
- ground black pepper, as required

1. In a large resealable bag, mix together the buttermilk, oil, garlic powder and 1 tablespoon of salt.
2. Add the whole chicken and seal the bag tightly.
3. Refrigerate to marinate for 24 hours up to 2 days.
4. Remove the chicken from bag and pat dry with paper towels.
5. Season the chicken with salt and black pepper.
6. with kitchen twine, tie off wings and legs.
7. When the cooking time is completed, open the oven door and place the chicken onto a cutting board for about 10 minutes before carving.

French-Inspired Chicken Stew

Prep time:10 minutes | Cook time: 60 minutes | Serves 6

- Meat from 1 rotisserie chicken, roughly shredded
- 1 (12-ounce) package precooked chicken sausages, sliced
- 3 medium carrots, diced
- 1 (16-ounce) bag frozen pearl onions
- 1 (15-ounce) can cannellini beans, drained and rinsed
- 3 garlic cloves, minced
- 2 cups chicken stock
- Kosher salt and freshly ground black pepper, to taste

1. In a large bowl, combine the chicken, sausages, carrots, pearl onions, beans, garlic, stock, salt, and pepper. Pour the mixture into a casserole dish.
2. Install a wire rack on Level 3. Select AIR ROAST, set the temperature to 325°F, and set the time to 60 minutes. Press START/STOP to begin preheating.
3. When the unit has preheated, place the casserole dish on the wire rack. Close the oven door to begin cooking.
4. When cooking is complete, let the stew cool for 10 minutes before serving.

Sweet and Sour Chicken Thighs

Prep time: 10 minutes | Cook time: 20 minutes| Serves 1

- ¼ tablespoon soy sauce
- ¼ tablespoon rice vinegar
- ½ teaspoon sugar
- ½ garlic, minced
- ½ scallion, finely chopped
- ¼ cup corn flour
- 1 chicken thigh, skinless and boneless
- Salt and black pepper, to taste

1. Take a bowl and mix all the ingredients together except chicken and corn flour.
2. Add the chicken thigh to the bowl to coat well.
3. Take another bowl and add corn flour.
4. Remove the chicken thighs from marinade and lightly coat with corn flour.
5. Turn on your Ninja Foodi and select "Air Fry".
6. Select the timer for about 10 minutes and temperature for 390 °F. Press START/STOP to begin preheating.
7. When the unit beeps to signify it has preheated, open the oven and place an air fry basket on Level 3.
8. Serve hot and enjoy!

Chapter 5

Beef, Pork and Lamb Recipes

Herbed Chuck Roast

Prep time: 5 minutes | Cook time: 45 minutes |Serves 6

- 1 beef chuck roast
- 1 tablespoon olive oil
- 1 teaspoon dried rosemary, crushed
- 1 teaspoon dried thyme, crushed
- Salt, as required

1. In a bowl, add the oil, herbs and salt and mix well.
2. Coat the beef roast with herb mixture generously.
3. Arrange the beef roast onto the greased SearPlate.
4. with a sharp knife, cut the beef roast into desired size slices and serve.

American Roast Beef

Prep time: 5 minutes | Cook time: 1 hour |Serves 3

- 1½ pounds beef eye of round roast
- ¼ teaspoon kosher salt
- ⅛ teaspoon black pepper, freshly ground
- ¼ teaspoon garlic powder

1. Turn on your Ninja Foodi and rotate the knob to select "Air Roast".
2. Preheat by selecting the timer for 3 minutes and temperature for 375 °F.
3. Place beef in a SearPlate and season with salt, garlic powder and pepper.
4. Roast in oven for about an hour.
5. Remove from oven and set aside for 10 minutes before slicing.
6. Serve warm and enjoy!

Ground Beef Casserole

Prep time: 5 minutes | Cook time: 25 minutes |Serves 3

- ¼ medium onion, chopped
- ½ pound extra lean ground beef
- ½ pound penne
- ½ tablespoon olive oil
- ½ cup marinara sauce
- 1 cup cheddar cheese, shredded
- Salt and pepper to taste

1. Take a large pot with lightly salted water and bring it to a boil. Add penne and let it cook for about 10 minutes.
2. Take a pan and add oil, beef and onion.
3. Fry for about 10 minutes over medium-high heat and add garlic.
4. Stir in the marinara sauce and add salt and pepper according to taste.
5. Add the beef-marinara mixture on top of the penne pasta. Lastly, add cheese with cheese.
6. Bake for about 10 minutes in preheated Ninja Foodi until the cheese is nicely melted.
7. Serve immediately.

Tarragon Beef Shanks

Prep time: 15 minutes | Cook time: 15 minutes | Serves 4

- 2 tablespoons olive oil
- 2 pounds beef shank
- salt and black pepper to taste
- 1 onion, diced
- 2 stalks celery, diced
- 1 cup Marsala wine
- 2 tablespoons dried tarragon

1. Place the beef shanks in a baking pan.
2. Whisk the rest of the ingredients in a bowl and pour over the shanks.
3. Place these shanks in the air fry basket.
4. Transfer the basket to the Ninja Foodi and close the door.
5. Select "Air Fry" mode by rotating the dial.
6. Press the TIME/SLICE button and change the value to 15 minutes
7. Press the TEMP/DARKNESS button and change the value to 375 °F.
8. Press Start/Pause to begin cooking.
9. Serve warm.

Sauce Glazed Meatloaf

Prep time: 15 minutes | Cook time: 60 minutes

Serves6

- 1 pound ground beef
- ½ onion chopped
- 1 egg
- 1 ½ garlic clove, minced
- 1 ½ tablespoons ketchup
- 1 ½ tablespoons fresh parsley, chopped
- ¼ cup breadcrumbs
- 2 tablespoons milk
- Salt to taste
- 1 ½ teaspoons herb seasoning
- ¼ teaspoon black pepper
- ½ teaspoon ground paprika
- ¾ cup ketchup
- 1 teaspoon garlic powder
- ½ teaspoon onion powder
- ¼ teaspoon ground black pepper
- ¼ teaspoon salt

1. Thoroughly mix ground beef with egg, onion, garlic, crumbs, and all the ingredients in a bowl.
2. Grease a meatloaf pan with oil or butter and spread the minced beef in the pan.
3. Stir cook for 5 minutes until it thickens.
4. Brush this glaze over the meatloaf and bake it again for 15 minutes.
5. Slice and serve.

Teriyaki Pork and Pineapple Skewers

Prep time: 10 minutes | Cook time: 12 minutes |

Serves 4

- ¼ teaspoon kosher salt or ⅛ teaspoon fine salt
- 1 medium pork tenderloin (about 1 pound), cut into 1½-inch chunks
- 1 red bell pepper, seeded and cut into 1-inch pieces
- 1 green bell pepper, seeded and cut into 1-inch pieces
- 2 cups fresh pineapple chunks
- ¾ cup Teriyaki Sauce or store-bought variety

1. Sprinkle the salt over the pork cubes.
2. Alternate the pork, bell peppers, and pineapple on the skewers, making about 12 skewers (if you use the larger skewers, you'll probably only need 8). Liberally brush the skewers with about half of the Teriyaki Sauce.
3. Select AIR ROAST, set temperature to 375°F, and set time to 10 minutes. Select START/PAUSE to begin preheating.
4. When cooking is complete, the vegetables should be tender and browned in spots, and the pork browned and cooked through. Remove the pan from the oven and serve.

Steak with Bell Peppers

Prep time: 15 minutes | Cook time: 11 minutes

Serves4

- 1 teaspoon dried oregano, crushed
- 1 teaspoon onion powder
- 1 teaspoon garlic powder
- 1 teaspoon red chili powder
- 1 teaspoon paprika
- Salt, as required
- 1¼ pounds flank steak, cut into thin strips
- 3 green bell peppers, seeded and cubed
- 1 red onion, sliced
- 2 tablespoons olive oil
- 3-4 tablespoons feta cheese, crumbled

1. In a large bowl, mix the oregano and spices together.
2. Add the steak strips, bell peppers, onion, and oil and mix until well combined.
3. Press "Power" button of Ninja Foodi and select "Air Fry" function.
4. Press TEMP/SHADE +/- buttons to set the temperature at 390 °F.
5. Serve immediately with the topping of feta.

Pork Chops with Cashew Sauce

Prep time: 15 minutes | Cook time: 52 minutes |

Serves 8

- 8 pork loin chops
- 1 small onion, peeled and chopped
- Salt and black pepper, to taste
- For Its Sauce:
- ¼ cup cashews, finely chopped
- 1 cup cashew butter
- 1 oz wheat flour
- 6 fl oz milk
- 6 fl oz beef stock
- 2 tablespoons coconut cream, whipping
- Salt and black pepper, to taste

1. Place the pork loin chops and onion in a baking tray, then drizzle salt and black pepper on top.
2. Transfer the tray to the 2nd rack position of Ninja Foodi and close the door.
3. Select the "Bake" Mode using the Function Keys and select Rack Level 2.
4. Set its cooking time to 45 minutes and temperature to 375 °F, then press "START/STOP" to initiate cooking.

Glazed Beef Short Ribs

**Prep time: 15 minutes | Cook time: 8 minutes |
Serves 4**

- 2 pounds bone-in beef short ribs
- 3 tablespoons scallions, chopped
- ½ tablespoon fresh ginger, finely grated
- ½ cup low-sodium soy sauce
- ¼ cup balsamic vinegar
- ½ tablespoon Sriracha
- 1 tablespoon sugar
- ½ teaspoon ground black pepper

1. In a resealable bag, place all the ingredients.
2. Seal the bag and shake to coat well.
3. Refrigerate overnight.
4. Press "Power" button of Ninja Foodi and turn the dial to select "Air Fry" mode.
5. Press TIME/SLICE button and again turn the dial to set the cooking time to 8 minutes
6. Now push TEMP/DARKNESS button and rotate the dial to set the temperature at 380 °F.
7. Press "Start/Pause" button to start.
8. Flip the ribs once halfway through.
9. When the cooking time is completed, open the oven door and serve hot.

Greek Lamb Farfalle

**Prep time: 5 minutes | Cook time: 20 minutes
|Serves 6**

- 1 tablespoon olive oil
- 1 onion, chopped
- 2 garlic cloves, chopped
- 2 teaspoons dried oregano
- 1 pound pack lamb mince
- ¾ pound tin tomatoes, chopped
- ¼ cup black olives pitted
- ½ cup frozen spinach, defrosted
- 2 tablespoons dill, removed and chopped
- 9 ounces farfalle paste, boiled
- 1 ball half-fat mozzarella, torn

1. Sauté onion and garlic with oil in a pan over moderate heat for 5 minutes.
2. Stir in tomatoes, spinach, dill, oregano, lamb, and olives, then stir cook for 5 minutes.
3. Spread the lamb in the SearPlate and toss in the boiled Farfalle pasta.
4. Top the pasta lamb mix with mozzarella cheese.
5. Transfer the SearPlate into Ninja Foodi and close the door.
6. Select "Air Fry" mode by rotating the dial.
7. Press Start/Stop to begin cooking.
8. Serve warm.

Lamb Rack with lemon Crust

Prep time: 15 minutes| Cook time: 25 minutes | Serves 3

- 1 ⅔ pounds frenched rack of lamb
- salt and black pepper, to taste
- ¼ pound dry breadcrumbs
- 1 teaspoon garlic, grated
- ½ teaspoon salt
- 1 teaspoon cumin seeds
- 1 teaspoon ground cumin
- ½ teaspoon grated lemon rind
- 1 egg, beaten

1. Place the lamb rack in a sheet pan and pour the whisked egg on top.
2. Whisk the rest of the crusting ingredients in a bowl and spread over the lamb.
3. Transfer the sheet pan to the Ninja Foodi and close the door.
4. Select "Air Fry" mode by rotating the dial.
5. Press the TIME/SLICE button and change the value to 25 minutes.
6. Press the TEMP/DARKNESS button and change the value to 350 °F.
7. Press Start/Pause to begin cooking.
8. Serve warm.

Simple Beef Tenderloin

Prep time: 10 minutes | Cook time: 50 minutes | Serves 10

- 1 (3½-pound) beef tenderloin, trimmed
- 2 tablespoons olive oil
- Salt and ground black pepper, as required

1. with kitchen twine, tie the tenderloin.
2. Rub the tenderloin with oil and season with salt and black pepper.
3. Place the tenderloin into the greased baking pan.
4. Press "Power Button" of Ninja Foodi and select the "Air Roast" function.
5. Press "Temp Button" to set the temperature at 400 °F.
6. Now press "time Button" to set the cooking time to 50 minutes.
7. Press "START/STOP" button to start.
8. When the unit beeps to show that it is preheated, open the lid and insert the baking pan in the oven.
9. When cooking time is completed, open the lid and place the tenderloin onto a platter for about 10 minutes before slicing.
10. with a sharp knife, cut the tenderloin into desired sized slices and serve.

Pork Wellington with Garlic Green Beans

Prep time:15 minutes | Cook time: 45 minutes | Serves 4 to 6

- 1 pound green beans, trimmed
- 2 tablespoons extra-virgin olive oil
- 2 garlic cloves, minced
- Kosher salt and freshly ground black pepper, to taste
- All-purpose flour, for dusting
- 1 frozen puff pastry sheet, thawed and rolled out to 12 by 15 inches
- 2 tablespoons Dijon mustard
- 1 large egg, beaten with 1 tablespoon water

1. In a large bowl, toss the green beans with the olive oil, garlic, salt, and pepper. Set aside.
2. Dust a clean work surface with flour and lay out the puff pastry. Gently spread the apricot preserves over the middle 2 quarters. Sprinkle with the thyme and a pinch of salt and pepper.
3. Layer the prosciutto on top of the preserves lengthwise; you want the prosciutto to wrap around the whole tenderloin.
4. Cooking is complete when the puff pastry is golden brown and an instant-read thermometer inserted into the pork reads at least 145°F.

Lamb Chops with Carrots

Prep time: 15 minutes | Cook time: 10 minutes | Serves 4

- 2 tablespoons fresh rosemary, minced
- 2 tablespoons fresh mint leaves, minced
- 1 garlic clove, minced
- 3 tablespoons olive oil
- salt and ground black pepper, as required
- 4 (6-ounce) lamb chops
- 2 large carrots, peeled and cubed

1. In a large bowl, mix together the herbs, garlic, oil, salt, and black pepper.
2. Add the chops and generously coat with mixture.
3. Refrigerate to marinate for about 3 hours.
4. In a large pan of water, soak the carrots for about 15 minutes
5. Drain the carrots completely.
6. Press "Power" button of Ninja Foodi and turn the dial to select "Air Fry" mode.
7. Press TIME/SLICE button and again turn the dial to set the cooking time to 10 minutes
8. Now push TEMP/DARKNESS button and rotate the dial to set the temperature at 390 °F.
9. Press "Start/Pause" button to start.
10. Serve hot.

Chapter 6

Fish and Seafood Recipes

Shrimp with Celery and Toasted Cashews

Prep time: 10 minutes | Cook time: 10 minutes | Serves 4

- 1 cup roasted, salted cashews
- ½ cup Asian-Style Sauce
- 1 tablespoon sesame oil
- ½ teaspoon red pepper flakes
- 1 teaspoon cornstarch
- 1 tablespoon dry sherry (optional)
- 1¼ pound medium shrimp (21–25 or 25–30 count), peeled and deveined

1. Place the cashews in the Air Fry basket.
2. Select AIR FRY, set temperature to 400°F, and set time to 25 minutes. Select START/PAUSE to begin preheating.
3. When cooking is complete, the shrimp should be pink and opaque. Remove the pan from the oven. Stir in the cashews and garnish with the remaining scallion greens. Serve with steamed rice, if desired.

Lemon Herb Fish Fillets

Prep time: 5 minutes | Cook time: 10 minutes |Serves 4

- 4 tilapia fillets
- 1 tsp lemon juice
- 1 tsp garlic powder
- 1 tsp dried oregano
- Pepper
- Salt

1. Select air fry mode set the temperature to 400 F and set the timer to 10 minutes. Press the setting dial to preheat.
2. In a small bowl, mix garlic powder, oregano, lemon juice, pepper, and salt.
3. Rub fish fillets with spice mixture and place into the air fryer basket.
4. Once the unit is preheated, open the door, and place the air fryer basket on the top level of the oven, and close the door.
5. Serve and enjoy.

Honey Mustard Salmon with Asparagus

Prep time: 10 minutes | Cook time: 15 minutes | Serves 4

- 4 (6-ounce) salmon fillets, with or without skin
- 1 tablespoon honey
- 2 teaspoons Dijon mustard
- Lemon wedges, for serving

1. Sprinkle the salmon on both sides with ½ teaspoon of kosher salt.
2. In a small bowl, whisk together the honey, mustard, and 1 tablespoon of butter.
3. When cooking is complete, remove the pan from the oven. Squeeze a little lemon juice over the fish and vegetables, and serve.

Broiled Scallops

Prep time: 5 minutes | Cook time: 8 minutes |Serves 2

- 1 pound bay scallops
- 1 tablespoon lemon juice
- 1 tablespoon butter, melted
- ½ tablespoon garlic salt

1. Turn on your Ninja Foodi and rotate the knob to select "Broil".
2. Rinse scallop and place in SearPlate.
3. Season with garlic salt, butter and lemon juice.
4. Select the timer for about 8 minutes and temperature for HI.
5. Remove from oven and serve warm.

Lemongrass Steamed Tuna

Prep time: 10 minutes | Cook time: 10 minutes |Serves 4

- 4 small tuna steaks
- 2 tablespoons low-sodium soy sauce
- 2 teaspoons sesame oil
- 2 teaspoons rice wine vinegar
- 1 teaspoon grated peeled fresh ginger
- ⅛ teaspoon freshly ground black pepper
- 1 stalk lemongrass, bent in half
- 3 tablespoons freshly squeezed lemon juice

1. Place the tuna steaks on a plate.
2. In a small bowl, whisk the soy sauce, sesame oil, vinegar, and ginger until combined. Let marinate for 10 minutes.
3. Select BAKE, set the temperature to 390°F, and set the time to 10 minutes. Select START/STOP to begin.
4. When the cooking is complete, a food thermometer inserted into the tuna should register at least 145°F. Discard the lemongrass and serve the tuna.

Air Fried Scallops

Prep time: 5 minutes | Cook time: 4 minutes Serves 4

- 16 scallops
- ¼teaspoon garlic powder
- 1 teaspoon olive oil
- Salt and pepper to taste

1. Add scallops and remaining ingredients into the mixing bowl and toss well. Add scallops to the Air Fryer basket.
2. Place the wire rack inside your Ninja Foodi.
3. Select "AIR CRISP" mode, set the temperature to 390 °F, and set the time to 4 minutes.
4. Press "START/PAUSE" to begin preheating.
5. Once the oven is preheated, place the Air Crisp Basket on the wire rack and close the oven door to start cooking. Cook for 4 minutes.
6. Serve and enjoy.

Garlic Butter Salmon Bites

Prep time: 6 minutes | Cook time: 10 minutes
Serves 2

- 1 tablespoon lemon juice
- 2 tablespoons butter
- ½ tablespoon garlic, minced
- ½ teaspoon pepper
- 4 ounces salmon
- ½ teaspoon salt
- ½ tablespoon apple cider or rice vinegar

1. Take a large bowl and add everything except salmon and whisk together until well combined.
2. Slice the salmon into small cubes and marinade them into the mixture.
3. Cover the bowl with plastic wrap and refrigerate it for about an hour.
4. Now, spread out the marinated salmon cubes into the air fry basket.
5. Turn on your Ninja Foodi and select "Air Fry".
6. Select the timer for 10 minutes and temperature for 350 °F.
7. Wait till the salmon is finely cooked.
8. Serve and enjoy!

Prawns in Butter Sauce

Prep time: 15 minutes | Cook time: 6 minutes |
Serves 2

- ½ pound large prawns, peeled and deveined
- 1 large garlic clove, minced
- 1 tablespoon butter, melted
- 1 teaspoon fresh lemon zest, grated

1. In a bowl, add all the ingredients and toss to coat well.
2. Set aside at room temperature for about 30 minutes
3. Arrange the prawn mixture into a sheet pan.
4. Press "Power" button of Ninja Foodi and turn the dial to select "Bake" mode.
5. Press TIME/SLICE button and again turn the dial to set the cooking time to 6 minutes
6. Now push TEMP/DARKNESS button and rotate the dial to set the temperature at 450 °F.
7. When cooking time is completed, open the oven door and serve immediately.

Tropical Mahi-Mahi and Vegetables

Prep time:15 minutes | Cook time: 25 to 30 minutes | Serves 6

- 2 cups baby carrots, halved
- 2 small russet potatoes, peeled and cut into ½-inch sticks
- 2 tablespoons crushed garlic
- 3 tablespoons canola oil, divided
- 1 small pineapple, peeled, cored, and cut into wedges
- 2 teaspoons curry powder, divided
- 6 (6-ounce) mahi-mahi fillets
- Juice of 1 lime
- Kosher salt and freshly ground black pepper, to taste

1. In a medium bowl, toss the carrots, potatoes, garlic, and 1 tablespoon of oil until evenly coated. Arrange the vegetables evenly in the air fryer basket.
2. In a separate bowl, toss the pineapple with 1 teaspoon of curry powder and arrange in the basket with the vegetables.
3. Cooking is complete when an instant-read thermometer inserted in the fish reads 145°F. Serve the fish with the vegetables and pineapple.

Ricotta Toasts with Salmon

Prep time: 10 minutes | Cook time: 4 minutes | Serves 2

- 4 bread slices
- 8 ounces ricotta cheese
- 1 teaspoon lemon zest
- freshly ground black pepper, to taste
- 4 ounces smoked salmon

1. In a food processor, add the garlic, ricotta, lemon zest and black pepper and pulse until smooth.
2. Spread ricotta mixture over each bread slices evenly.
3. Press "Power" button of Ninja Foodi and turn the dial to select "Air Fry" mode.
4. Press TIME/SLICE button and again turn the dial to set the cooking time to 4 minutes
5. Now push TEMP/DARKNESS button and rotate the dial to set the temperature at 355 °F.
6. Press "Start/Pause" button to start.
7. When cooking time is completed, open the oven door and transfer the slices onto serving plates.
8. Top with salmon and serve.

Beer-Battered Fish and Chips

Prep time: 5 minutes | Cook time: 30 minutes |Serves 4

- 1 cup all-purpose flour
- ½ cup cornstarch
- 1 teaspoon garlic powder
- Salt
- Freshly ground black pepper
- 2 eggs
- 4 (4-ounce) cod fillets
- Cooking oil spray
- 1 recipe Classic French Fries

1. In a medium bowl, stir together the flour, cornstarch, and garlic powder, and season with salt and pepper.
2. In a medium bowl, beat the eggs with the beer.
3. Dip each cod fillet in the flour-cornstarch mixture and then in the egg-beer mixture. Dip the cod in the flour and cornstarch a second time.
4. Repeat steps 5, 6, and 7 for the remaining fillets.
5. When the cooking is complete, serve with Classic French Fries.

Fish in Yogurt Marinade

Prep time: 15 minutes | Cook time: 10 minutes | Serves 2

- 1 cup plain Greek yogurt
- Finely grated zest of 1 lemon
- 1 tablespoon lemon juice
- 1 tablespoon finely minced garlic
- 3 tablespoons fresh oregano leaves
- 1 teaspoon ground cumin
- ¼ teaspoon ground allspice
- ½ teaspoon salt
- ½ teaspoon freshly ground black pepper
- 1½ pounds perch filets

1. Mix lemon zest, yogurt, garlic, cumin, oregano, black pepper, salt, and allspices in a shallow pan.
2. Add fish to this marinade, mix well to coat then cover it with a plastic wrap.
3. Marinate for 15 minutes in the refrigerator, then uncover.
4. Select the "Bake" Mode using the Function Keys and select Rack Level 2.
5. Set its cooking time to 10 minutes and temperature to 450 °F, then press "START/STOP" to initiate cooking.
6. Serve warm.

Fish Newburg with Haddock

Prep time: 15 minutes | Cook time: 29 minutes

Serves4

- 1 ½ pounds haddock fillets
- Salt and freshly ground black pepper
- 4 tablespoons butter
- 1 tablespoon 2 teaspoons flour
- ¼ teaspoon sweet paprika
- ¼ teaspoon ground nutmeg
- Dash cayenne pepper
- ¾ cup heavy cream
- ½ cup milk
- 3 tablespoons dry sherry
- 2 large egg yolks

1. Rub haddock with black pepper and salt, then place in a sheet pan.
2. Place the spiced haddock in the pastry shell and close it like a calzone.
3. Drizzle 1 tablespoon of melted butter on top.
4. Cook the mixture on low heat for 2 minutes.
5. Add the baked wrapped haddock to its sauce and cook until warm.
6. Serve warm.

Scallops with Capers Sauce

Prep time: 10 minutes | Cook time: 6 minutes |

Serves 2

- 10 (1-ounce) sea scallops, cleaned and patted very dry
- Salt and ground black pepper, as required
- ¼ cup extra-virgin olive oil
- 2 tablespoons fresh parsley, finely chopped
- 2 teaspoons capers, finely chopped
- 1 teaspoon fresh lemon zest, finely grated
- ½ teaspoon garlic, finely chopped

1. Season each scallop evenly with salt and black pepper.
2. Press "Power Button" of Ninja Foodi and select "Air Fry" function.
3. Press "Temp Button" to set the temperature at 400 °F.
4. Now press "time Button" to set the cooking time to 6 minutes.
5. Press "START/STOP" button to start.
6. When the unit beeps to show that it is preheated, open the lid and grease the air fry basket.
7. Top with the sauce and serve immediately.

Salmon & Asparagus Parcel

Prep time: 15 minutes | Cook time: 13 minutes |
Serves 2

- 2 (4-ounce) salmon fillets
- 6 asparagus stalks
- ¼ cup white sauce
- 1 teaspoon oil
- ¼ cup champagne
- salt and ground black pepper, as required

1. In a bowl, mix together all the ingredients.
2. Divide the salmon mixture over 2 pieces of foil evenly.
3. Seal the foil around the salmon mixture to form the packet.
4. Press "Power" button of Ninja Foodi and turn the dial to select "Air Fry" mode.
5. Press TIME/SLICE button and again turn the dial to set the cooking time to 13 minutes
6. Now push TEMP/DARKNESS button and rotate the dial to set the temperature at 355 °F.
7. When cooking time is completed, open the oven door and serve hot.

Fish Casserole

Prep time: 5 minutes | Cook time: 40 minutes |
Serves 3

- ½ tablespoon unsalted butter, softened
- ¼ teaspoon salt
- 1 pound white fish fillet
- ¼ teaspoon pepper
- ½ sweet onion, thinly sliced
- 2 teaspoons extra-virgin olive oil, divided
- ¼ teaspoon dry thyme
- 1 pinch nutmeg
- ¼ teaspoon paprika
- 1/8 teaspoon garlic powder
- ½ cup shredded Swiss cheese

1. Turn on your Ninja Foodi and rotate the knob to select "Bake".
2. Preheat by selecting the timer for 3 minutes and temperature for 400 °F.
3. Arrange fish fillet on a dish and season with salt and pepper.
4. Take a pan and heat oil over medium-high heat. Add onion and cook until it starts to brown.
5. Select the timer for about 18 to 22 minutes and temperature for 400 °F.
6. Serve warm.

Chapter 7

Vegetables and Sides Recipes

Broccoli with Cauliflower

Prep time: 5 minutes | Cook time: 20 minutes |Serves 4

- 1½ cups broccoli, cut into 1-inch pieces
- 1½ cups cauliflower, cut into 1-inch pieces
- 1 tablespoon olive oil
- Salt, as required

1. In a bowl, add the vegetables, oil, and salt and toss to coat well.
2. Press AIR OVEN MODE button of Ninja Foodi and turn the dial to select "Air Fry" mode.
3. Press TIME/SLICES button and again turn the dial to set the cooking time to 20 minutes.
4. Now push TEMP/SHADE button and rotate the dial to set the temperature at 375 °F.
5. Press "Start/Stop" button to start.
6. When the unit beeps to show that it is preheated, open the oven door.
7. Arrange the veggie mixture into the greased air fry basket and insert in the oven.
8. When cooking time is completed, open the oven door and serve hot.

Savory Roasted Sweet Potatoes

Prep time: 10 minutes | Cook time: 25 minutes |Serves 4

- Cooking oil spray
- 2 sweet potatoes, peeled and cut into 1-inch cubes
- Freshly ground black pepper
- ½ teaspoon dried thyme
- ½ teaspoon dried marjoram
- ¼ cup grated Parmesan cheese

1. Insert the crisper plate into the basket and the basket into the unit. Preheat the unit by selecting AIR ROAST, setting the temperature to 330°F, and setting the time to 3 minutes. Select START/STOP to begin.
2. Once the unit is preheated, spray the crisper plate with cooking oil. Put the sweet potato cubes into the basket and drizzle with olive oil. Toss gently to coat. Sprinkle with the salt, pepper, thyme, and marjoram and toss again.
3. When the cooking is complete, the potatoes should be tender. Serve immediately.

Brussels Sprouts Gratin

Prep time: 5 minutes | Cook time: 35 minutes |Serves 6

- 1 pound Brussels sprouts
- 1 garlic clove, cut in half
- 3 tablespoons butter, divided
- 2 tablespoons shallots, minced
- 2 tablespoons all-purpose flour
- Kosher salt, to taste
- Freshly ground black pepper
- 1 dash ground nutmeg
- 1 cup milk
- ½ cup fontina cheese, shredded
- 1 strip of bacon, cooked and crumbled
- ½ cup fine bread crumbs

1. Trim the Brussels sprouts and remove their outer leaves.
2. Slice the sprouts into quarters, then rinse them under cold water.
3. Grease a gratin dish with cooking spray and rub it with garlic halves.
4. Boil salted water in a suitable pan, then add Brussels sprouts.
5. Cook the sprouts for 3 minutes, then immediately drain.
6. Press Start/Stop to begin cooking.
7. Enjoy!

Feta and Vegetable Bake

Prep time: 15 minutes | Cook time: 30 minutes | Serves 4

- ½ cup brown rice, cooked
- 5 ounces feta cheese, cubed
- 2 tablespoons olive oil
- 2 tablespoons basil, dried
- 2 tablespoons parsley, dried
- 1 garlic clove
- 1 onion, julienned
- 1 bell pepper, red, julienned
- 2 good handful cherry tomatoes
- 1 jalapeño, chopped
- 1 handful olives, sliced
- 10 tablespoons water

1. Spread the cheese in a sheet pan and drizzle half of the herbs on top.
2. Toss remaining vegetables with rice and water, spread over the cheese.
3. Add remaining herbs on top and spread them evenly.
4. Transfer the pan to the Ninja Foodi and close the door.
5. Select "Bake" mode by rotating the dial.
6. Press the TEMP/DARKNESS button and change the value to 350 °F.
7. Serve warm.

Asparagus with Garlic and Parmesan

Prep time: 5 minutes | Cook time: 10 minutes
Serves 4

- 1 bundle asparagus
- 1 teaspoon olive oil
- ⅛ teaspoon garlic salt
- 1 tablespoon parmesan cheese
- Pepper to taste

1. Clean the asparagus and dry it. To remove the woody stalks, cut 1 inch off the bottom.
2. In a sheet pan, arrange asparagus in a single layer and spray with oil.
3. On top of the asparagus, evenly sprinkle garlic salt. Season with salt and pepper, then sprinkle with Parmesan cheese.
4. Turn on Ninja Foodi and select "Air Fry".
5. Select the timer for 10 minutes and the temperature for 350 °F.
6. When the unit beeps to signify it has preheated, open the oven and place the sheet pan onto Level 3 in oven. Close the oven and let it cook.
7. Enjoy right away.

Broccoli Cheese Casserole

Prep time: 15 minutes | Cook time: 30 minutes
|Serves 10

- 2 bunches broccoli
- ¼ cup water
- 1 large egg, lightly beaten
- 10½ ounces cream of chicken soup
- ½ cup mayonnaise
- ½ cup sour cream
- 1 teaspoon salt
- For the topping:
- 1 cup Ritz crackers, crushed
- 2 tablespoons butter, melted

1. Insert a wire rack on Level 3. Select the BAKE function, 350°F, for 30 minutes. While the oven is preheating, prepare an air fryer-safe casserole dish with non-stick spray.
2. When the unit beeps to signify it has preheated, open the oven and insert the oven-safe casserole dish on the wire rack Bake for 20 minutes
3. Meanwhile, in a small bowl, mix the crackers and butter. Take the casserole out of the oven and sprinkle with the topping. Cook for another 10 minutes.

Breaded Artichoke Hearts

Prep time: 15 minutes | Cook time: 8 minutes |Serves 4

- 12 whole artichoke hearts packed in water, drained
- ½ cup all-purpose flour
- 1 egg
- ⅓ cup panko bread crumbs
- 1 teaspoon Italian seasoning
- Cooking oil spray

1. Squeeze any excess water from the artichoke hearts and place them on paper towels to dry.
2. Place the flour in a small bowl.
3. In another small bowl, beat the egg.
4. In a third small bowl, stir together the panko and Italian seasoning.
5. Dip the artichoke hearts in the flour, in the egg, and into the panko mixture until coated.
6. When the cooking is complete, the artichoke hearts should be deep golden brown and crisp. Cool for 5 minutes before serving.

Caramelized Baby Carrots

Prep time: 5 minutes | Cook time: 15 minutes |Serves 4

- ½ cup butter, melted
- ½ cup brown sugar
- 1 pound bag baby carrots

1. In a bowl, mix together the butter, brown sugar and carrots.
2. Press AIR OVEN MODE button of Ninja Foodi and turn the dial to select "Air Fry" mode.
3. Press TIME/SLICES button and again turn the dial to set the cooking time to 15 minutes.
4. Now push TEMP/SHADE button and rotate the dial to set the temperature at 400 °F.
5. Press "Start/Stop" button to start.
6. When the unit beeps to show that it is preheated, open the oven door.
7. Arrange the carrots in a greased air fry basket and insert in the oven.
8. When cooking time is completed, open the oven door and serve warm.

Beans & Veggie Burgers

Prep time: 15 minutes | Cook time: 22 minutes | Serves 4

- 1 cup cooked black beans
- 2 cups boiled potatoes, peeled and mashed
- 1 cup fresh spinach, chopped
- 1 cup fresh mushrooms, chopped
- 2 teaspoons Chile lime seasoning

1. In a large bowl, add the beans, potatoes, spinach, mushrooms, and seasoning and with your hands, mix until well combined.
2. Make 4 equal-sized patties from the mixture.
3. Press "Power Button" of Ninja Foodi and select "Air Fry" function.
4. Press "Temp Button" to set the temperature at 370 °F.
5. Now press "time Button" to set the cooking time to 22 minutes.
6. Press "START/STOP" button to start.
7. When the unit beeps to show that it is preheated, open the lid.
8. Serve warm.

Crispy Bean and Cheese Tacos

Prep time: 12 minutes | Cook time: 7 minutes | Serves 4

- 1 (15-ounce) can black beans, drained and rinsed
- ½ cup prepared salsa (I use Frontera brand Double Roasted Salsa)
- 1½ teaspoons chili powder
- 2 tablespoons minced onion
- 4 ounces grated Monterey Jack cheese (plain or with jalapeños)
- Shredded lettuce, for serving

1. Place the beans in a medium bowl, preferably one with a flat bottom. Add the salsa and chili powder. Using a potato masher, coarsely mash the beans and salsa. Add the onion and cheese and stir to combine.
2. Select AIR FRY, set temperature to 400°F, and set time to 7 minutes. Select START/PAUSE to begin preheating.
3. Once the unit has preheated, slide the pan into the oven.

Cheesy Green Bean Casserole

Prep time: 5 minutes | Cook time: 35 minutes |Serves 6

- 4 cups green beans, cooked and chopped
- 3 tablespoons butter
- 8 ounces mushrooms, sliced
- ¼ cup onion, chopped
- 2 tablespoons flour
- 1 teaspoon salt
- ¼ teaspoon ground black pepper
- 1 ½ cups milk
- 2 cups cheddar cheese, shredded
- 2 tablespoons sour cream
- 1 cup soft breadcrumbs
- 2 tablespoons butter, melted
- ¼ cup Parmesan cheese, grated
- 1 cup French fried onions

1. Add butter to a suitable saucepan and melt it over medium-low heat.
2. Toss in onion and mushrooms, then sauté until soft.
3. Stir in flour, salt, and black pepper. Mix well, then slowly pour in the milk.
4. Stir in sour cream, green beans, and cheddar cheese, then cook until it thickens.
5. Press Start/Stop to begin cooking.
6. Serve and enjoy!

Roasted Vegetables

Prep time: 15 minutes | Cook time: 15 minutes | Serves 6

- 2 medium bell peppers cored, chopped
- 2 medium carrots, peeled and sliced
- 1 small zucchini, ends trimmed, sliced
- 1 medium broccoli, florets
- ½ red onion, peeled and diced
- 2 tablespoons olive oil
- 1 ½ teaspoons Italian seasoning
- 2 garlic cloves, minced
- Salt and freshly ground black pepper
- 1 cup grape tomatoes
- 1 tablespoon fresh lemon juice

1. Toss all the veggies with olive oil, Italian seasoning, salt, black pepper, and garlic in a large salad bowl.
2. Spread this broccoli-zucchini mixture in the sheet pan.
3. Transfer the pan to the 2nd rack position of Ninja Foodi and close the door.
4. Select the "Bake" Mode using the Function Keys and select Rack Level 2.
5. Set its cooking time to 15 minutes and temperature to 400 °F, then press "START/STOP" to initiate cooking.
6. Serve warm with lemon juice on top.
7. Enjoy.

Coconut Curried Tofu and Vegetables

Prep time:20 minutes | Cook time: 25 minutes | Serves 6 to 8

- 2 tablespoons soy sauce
- 1 tablespoon maple syrup
- 2 tablespoons curry powder
- 1 pound firm tofu, cut into 1-inch cubes
- ¼ cup unsweetened shredded coconut
- 1 head cauliflower, cut into 1-inch florets
- 1 (15-ounce) can chickpeas, drained and rinsed
- 1 (13-ounce) can coconut cream
- Canola oil cooking spray

1. In a bowl, combine the soy sauce, maple syrup, and curry powder. Place the tofu cubes in a resealable bag and pour in the marinade. Seal the bag and let the tofu marinate for 30 minutes at room temperature.
2. Put the coconut in a medium bowl. Remove the tofu cubes from the bag, reserving the marinade, and dredge the tofu in the coconut.
3. When cooking is complete, transfer the tofu to a serving dish. Top with the cauliflower mixture and drizzle with the reserved coconut sauce. Serve immediately.

Vegan Cakes

Prep time: 15 minutes | Cook time: 15 minutes | Serves 8

- 4 potatoes, diced and boiled
- 1 bunch green onions
- 1 lime, zest, and juice
- 1½-inch knob of fresh ginger
- 1 tablespoon tamari
- 4 tablespoons red curry paste
- 4 sheets nori
- 1 (398 grams) can heart of palm, drained
- ¾ cup canned artichoke hearts, drained
- black pepper, to taste
- salt, to taste

1. Add potatoes, green onions, lime zest, juice, and the rest of the ingredients to a food processor.
2. Press the pulse button and blend until smooth.
3. Make 8 small patties out of this mixture.
4. Place the patties in the air fry basket.
5. Transfer the basket to the Ninja Foodi and close the door.
6. Select "Air Fry" mode by rotating the dial.
7. Press Start/Pause to begin cooking.
8. Serve warm.

Chapter 8

Dessert Recipes

Chocolate Chip Cookies

Prep time: 5 minutes | Cook time: 45 minutes |Serves 4

- ½ cup butter, melted
- ¼ cup packed brown sugar
- ¼ cup granulated sugar
- 1 large egg
- 1 teaspoon pure vanilla extract
- 1½ cups all-purpose flour
- ½ teaspoon baking soda
- ½ teaspoon kosher salt
- ½ teaspoon chocolate chips

1. Whisk together melted butter and sugars in a medium mixing bowl. Whisk in the egg and vanilla extract until fully combined.
2. Combine the flour, baking soda, and salt.
3. Allow cooling for two minutes before serving.

Chocolate Cake

Prep time: 5 minutes | Cook time: 10 minutes |Serves 4

- 3 ½ oz butter, melted
- 3 ½ tablespoon sugar
- 1 ½ tablespoon self-rising flour
- 3 ½ oz dark chocolate, melted
- 2 eggs

1. Grease 4 ramekins with butter.
2. Preheat Ninja Foodi on "BAKE" function at 375 °F.
3. Beat the eggs and sugar until frothy.
4. Stir in butter and chocolate; gently fold in the flour. Divide the mixture between the ramekins and bake for 10 minutes.
5. Let cool for 2 minutes before turning the cakes upside down onto serving plates.

Roasted Bananas

Prep time: 5 minutes | Cook time: 7 minutes |Serves 1

- 1 banana, sliced
- Avocado oil for cooking spray

1. Using parchment paper, line the air fry basket.
2. Place banana slices in the air fry basket, making sure they do not touch.
3. Mist banana slices with avocado oil.
4. Turn on Ninja Foodi and rotate the knob to select "Air Roast".
5. Select the timer for 5 minutes and the temperature for 370 °F.
6. Remove the banana slices from the basket and carefully flip them.
7. Cook for another 3 minutes, or until the banana slices are browning and caramelized. Remove from the basket with care.
8. Allow cooling for two minutes before serving.

Fudge Brownies

Prep time: 15 minutes | Cook time: 20 minutes | Serves 8

- 1 cup sugar
- ½ cup butter, melted
- ½ cup flour
- ⅓ cup cocoa powder
- 1 teaspoon baking powder
- 2 eggs
- 1 teaspoon vanilla extract

1. Grease a baking pan.
2. In a large bowl, add the sugar and butter and whisk until light and fluffy.
3. Add the remaining ingredients and mix until well combined.
4. Place mixture into the prepared pan and with the back of a spatula, smooth the top surface.
5. Press "Power" button of Ninja Foodi and turn the dial to select "Air Fry" mode.
6. Cut into 8 equal-sized squares and serve.

Cherry Clafoutis

Prep time: 15 minutes | Cook time: 25 minutes | Serves 4

- 1½ cups fresh cherries, pitted
- 3 tablespoons vodka
- ¼ cup flour
- 2 tablespoons sugar
- pinch of salt
- ½ cup sour cream
- 1 egg
- 1 tablespoon butter
- ¼ cup powdered sugar

1. In a bowl, mix together the cherries and vodka.
2. In another bowl, mix together the flour, sugar, and salt.
3. Add the sour cream, and egg and mix until a smooth dough forms.
4. Grease a cake pan.
5. Place flour mixture evenly into the prepared cake pan.
6. Spread cherry mixture over the dough.
7. Place butter on top in the form of dots.
8. Now, invert the Clafoutis onto a platter and sprinkle with powdered sugar.
9. Cut the Clafoutis into desired sized slices and serve warm.

Carrot Mug Cake

Prep time: 10 minutes | Cook time: 20 minutes | Serves 1

- ¼ cup whole-wheat pastry flour
- 1 tablespoon coconut sugar
- ¼ teaspoon baking powder
- ⅛ teaspoon ground cinnamon
- ⅛ teaspoon ground ginger
- pinch of ground cloves
- pinch of ground allspice
- 1 tablespoon raisins
- 2 teaspoons applesauce

1. In a bowl, mix together the flour, sugar, baking powder, spices and salt.
2. Add the remaining ingredients and mix until well combined.
3. Place the mixture into a lightly greased ramekin.
4. Press "Power" button of Ninja Foodi and turn the dial to select the "Bake" mode.
5. Press TIME/SLICE button and again turn the dial to set the cooking time to 20 minutes
6. When cooking time is completed, open the oven door and place the ramekin onto a wire rack to cool slightly before serving.

Razzleberry Hand Pies

Prep time:15 minutes | Cook time: 25 minutes | Serves 6

- 1 (7.5-ounce) roll store-bought pie dough
- ½ cup frozen blackberries
- ½ cup frozen raspberries
- 1 teaspoon freshly squeezed lemon juice
- 1 teaspoon vanilla extract
- 3 tablespoons granulated sugar, plus 2 teaspoons
- 1 tablespoon cornstarch
- ¼ teaspoon ground cinnamon
- 2 tablespoons whole milk

1. Unroll the pie dough and use a 4½-inch round biscuit cutter to cut 4 circles of dough, then reroll the scrap dough to the same thickness and cut out 2 more circles of dough.
2. In a small bowl, combine the blackberries and raspberries with the lemon juice and vanilla, and toss to coat the berries. This will help the sugar mixture stick.
3. When cooking is complete, remove the pan from the oven and let the hand pies cool.

Salted Butter Pecan Cookies

Prep time:25 minutes | Cook time: 10 minutes | Serves 4

- 1½ cups pecan halves
- 1⅓ cups granulated sugar, divided
- ⅓ cup packed dark brown sugar
- 12 tablespoons (1½ sticks) unsalted butter, at room temperature
- 1¾ teaspoons kosher salt, divided
- 1 large egg
- 2 cups all-purpose flour
- 1½ cups toffee bits or butterscotch chips

1. Spread the pecans in a single layer on the sheet pan.
2. Install a wire rack on Level 2. Select BAKE, set the temperature to 350°F, and set the time to 6 minutes. Press START/STOP to begin preheating.
3. When the unit has preheated, place the sheet pan on the wire rack. Close the oven door to begin cooking.
4. Cooking is complete when the cookies are crisp and brown at the edges and soft in the center. Carefully remove the sheet pans and place on trivets for the cookies to cool before serving.

Walnut Brownies

Prep time: 15 minutes | Cook time: 22 minutes | Serves 4

- ½ cup chocolate, roughly chopped
- ⅓ cup butter
- 5 tablespoons sugar
- 1 egg, beaten
- 1 teaspoon vanilla extract
- pinch of salt
- 5 tablespoons self-rising flour
- ¼ cup walnuts, chopped

1. In a microwave-safe bowl, add the chocolate and butter. Microwave on high heat for about 2 minutes, stirring after every 30 seconds.
2. Remove from microwave and set aside to cool.
3. In another bowl, add the sugar, egg, vanilla extract, and salt and whisk until creamy and light.
4. Add the chocolate mixture and whisk until well combined.
5. Add the flour, and walnuts and mix until well combined.
6. Line a baking pan with a greased parchment paper.
7. Cut into 4 equal-sized squares and serve.

Peanut Brittle Bars

Prep time: 15 minutes | Cook time: 28 minutes | Serves 6

- 1 ½ cups all-purpose flour
- ½ cup whole wheat flour
- 1 cup packed brown sugar
- 1 teaspoon baking soda
- ¼ teaspoon salt
- 1 cup butter
- Topping
- 1 cup milk chocolate chips
- 2 cups salted peanuts
- 12 ¼ ounces caramel ice cream topping
- 3 tablespoons all-purpose flour

1. Mix flours with salt, baking soda, and brown sugar in a large bowl.
2. Spread the batter in a greased sheet pan.
3. Transfer the pan to the 2nd rack position of Ninja Foodi and close the door.
4. Select the "Air Fry" Mode using the Function Keys and select Rack Level 2.
5. Mix flour with caramels topping in a bowl and spread on top,
6. Bake again for 16 minutes.
7. Serve.

Appendix 1 Measurement Conversion Chart

Volume Equivalents (Dry)	
US STANDARD	METRIC (APPROXIMATE)
1/8 teaspoon	0.5 mL
1/4 teaspoon	1 mL
1/2 teaspoon	2 mL
3/4 teaspoon	4 mL
1 teaspoon	5 mL
1 tablespoon	15 mL
1/4 cup	59 mL
1/2 cup	118 mL
3/4 cup	177 mL
1 cup	235 mL
2 cups	475 mL
3 cups	700 mL
4 cups	1 L

Volume Equivalents (Liquid)		
US STANDARD	US STANDARD (OUNCES)	METRIC (APPROXIMATE)
2 tablespoons	1 fl.oz.	30 mL
1/4 cup	2 fl.oz.	60 mL
1/2 cup	4 fl.oz.	120 mL
1 cup	8 fl.oz.	240 mL
1 1/2 cup	12 fl.oz.	355 mL
2 cups or 1 pint	16 fl.oz.	475 mL
4 cups or 1 quart	32 fl.oz.	1 L
1 gallon	128 fl.oz.	4 L

Temperatures Equivalents	
FAHRENHEIT(F)	CELSIUS(C) APPROXIMATE)
225 °F	107 °C
250 °F	120 ° °C
275 °F	135 °C
300 °F	150 °C
325 °F	160 °C
350 °F	180 °C
375 °F	190 °C
400 °F	205 °C
425 °F	220 °C
450 °F	235 °C
475 °F	245 °C
500 °F	260 °C

Weight Equivalents	
US STANDARD	METRIC (APPROXIMATE)
1 ounce	28 g
2 ounces	57 g
5 ounces	142 g
10 ounces	284 g
15 ounces	425 g
16 ounces (1 pound)	455 g
1.5 pounds	680 g
2 pounds	907 g

Appendix 2 The Dirty Dozen and Clean Fifteen

The Environmental Working Group (EWG) is a nonprofit, nonpartisan organization dedicated to protecting human health and the environment Its mission is to empower people to live healthier lives in a healthier environment. This organization publishes an annual list of the twelve kinds of produce, in sequence, that have the highest amount of pesticide residue-the Dirty Dozen-as well as a list of the fifteen kinds ofproduce that have the least amount of pesticide residue-the Clean Fifteen.

THE DIRTY DOZEN	
The 2016 Dirty Dozen includes the following produce. These are considered among the year's most important produce to buy organic:	

Strawberries	Spinach
Apples	Tomatoes
Nectarines	Bell peppers
Peaches	Cherry tomatoes
Celery	Cucumbers
Grapes	Kale/collard greens
Cherries	Hot peppers

The Dirty Dozen list contains two additional itemskale/collard greens and hot peppers-because they tend to contain trace levels of highly hazardous pesticides.

THE CLEAN FIFTEEN	
The least critical to buy organically are the Clean Fifteen list. The following are on the 2016 list:	

Avocados	Papayas
Corn	Kiw
Pineapples	Eggplant
Cabbage	Honeydew
Sweet peas	Grapefruit
Onions	Cantaloupe
Asparagus	Cauliflower
Mangos	

Some of the sweet corn sold in the United States are made from genetically engineered (GE) seedstock. Buy organic varieties of these crops to avoid GE produce.

Appendix 3 Index

Adrienne S. Mackey

Made in United States
Troutdale, OR
02/12/2024